More Praise for *Feast of th...*

In *Feast of the Seven Fishes*, Linda Lamenza u...
language to invite us into her Italian Americ... ...and now
that childhood informs and colors her experiences as a woman, mother
and teacher. *When it is dark and no one / cares where we are*, what can we
come to understand about ourselves, one another and the world? This
compelling collection reads like snapshots of moments in time; however, many of them speak to complex and universal questions about
family and memory, patterns, time and resilience. Every poem inspires
curiosity about *the shrapnel of childhood / that pressure cooker* and how we
navigate our lives when we are released.
— Joan Kwon Glass, author of *Daughter of Three Gone Kingdoms*

At turns funny and poignant, tender and wise, *Feast of the Seven Fishes*
explores the small miracles in the ordinary, and the harder truths beneath. A Crown Royal bottle is repurposed for olive oil, an errand
to a fish market sets a child to wonder where they come from, an
aging mother shoplifts in the sewing store, an Asian ladybug's thirst is
quenched by strategically placed Pyrex water bowls, Lady Liberty, fed
up with tourists, whines she is bored looking at Brooklyn. Lamenza's
poems artfully narrate the whole of a life with control and craft, unveiling the complexities of a girlhood of Catholic school, Italian grandparents, and a drunken father, being mothered and mothering, being loved
and loving, and in every case, always reaching toward joy.
— Julia Lisella, author of *Our Lively Kingdom*

FEAST OF THE SEVEN FISHES

LINDA LAMENZA

Nixes Mate Books
Allston, Massachusetts

Copyright © 2024 Linda Lamenza

Book design by d'Entremont
Cover photograph used with permission.

All rights reserved. This book or any portion thereof may not be reproduced or used in any manner whatsoever without the express written permission of the publisher except for the use of brief quotations in a book review or scholarly journal.

Library of Congress Control Number: 2024902578

ISBN 978-1-949279-52-8

Nixes Mate Books
POBox 1179
Allston, MA 02134
nixesmate.pub

*For my parents, Rita Iachini Lamenza,
and Vincent James Lamenza.*

CONTENTS

COLAZIONE

Grey Advertising, 1956	3
Because My Father was Drunk By Noon	5
Self Portrait, Age 3	7
Yorktown Heights	8
Act of Contrition	9
Incident at Roseto	10
My Mother's Pane di Spagna	12
Metro-North Kid	13
Parenting Styles	14
If I Knew Who	15
Winter Polaroid	16
Spring Polaroid	17
Summer Polaroid	18
Fall Polaroid	19
My Grandparents: Angie and Frankie	20
Life Advice from My Mother	22
Poem Written By My Grandfather	24
Christening Heirloom	25
My Mother's Pane Di Pasqua	26
Sister Theresa's Class, 1977	27
Salve Regina	29
In the Garden of My Childhood	30
Feast of the Seven Fishes	31

PRANZO

In Praise of Vanity	34
Tadpoles	36
Independence Day	37
Pasta Sonata for Eight	38
Regarding Umbrellas	39
Skating Rink	40
Fire Pit	42
Love Poem for Best	43
Another Love Poem	44
No Need for Alarm	46
American Studies in Siena	47
Aubade for My Father	48
From the Closet in the Spare Bedroom	49
50th Birthday	50
Elegy for My Cousin	51
Amawalk Hill Cemetery: Visit No. 198	52
Easter Lunch	54
Undeliverable	55
Disequilibrium	56
A Freezing Sunday in May	57
While Gardening	58
Farmer's Market, Gratz, Pennsylvania	59
Tarot Cards	60
Provincetown	61
I Text My Sister	62

After School Lesson, Lexington Montessori School   63
Irregular Ode to Loud Internal Dialogue   64
A Few Brief Comments   65
When Spring Turns Back to Winter   66
And Perhaps in the Spring   68

CENA

Under the Centerville Bridge   70
Lady Liberty   71
TO: School Board RE: Remote Teaching, Fall 2020   72
Sourdough   73
At the Middlesex County Courthouse   75
Poem with No Regret   76
Deconstructing the Ash   77
Pandemic Potatoes   79
Cooking with My Stepdaughter   80
In the Game-On Café   82
Wintering   83
Invitation to Tea at Grand Rita's   85
My Mother Insists on Making Curtains   86
Climbing Wall   87
Poem with No Poet   88
A Cento   89
Splashdown, August 2020   91
Revenant   92
Learner's Permit   93
First Semester Freshman Year   95

Gap Year	96
Purple Haze	98
Sound Bath at Nicolette's	99
To Make the Dressing	100
View from The Inn at Mills Falls	101
Cleaning Out The Sock Drawer	103
St. Mary of Carmen Society Annual Italian-American Festival	104

FEAST OF THE SEVEN FISHES

COLAZIONE

GREY ADVERTISING, 1956

I am merely a machine,
tap out letters all day long,
can't even shift
my weight. She pounds

on my keys from 9 to 5 –
Ding!
A brief respite at 12:30.
(I love the silence after

Lunch.)
Too-fast-typing
makes my strikers stick.
Yesterday I spat out

invoices, all official,
with DUE DATE
underscored.
Today, office memos.

Nearly fell asleep on
the 12th one.
Weary,
work hours,

craving a freshly
inked ribbon.
Stillness is my balm.
My favorite time: 5:01.

BECAUSE MY FATHER WAS DRUNK BY NOON

Mom says *Hurry. Get ready.*
I am eight. I have to.
She gathers a picnic: a can of Progresso
Eggplant Appetizer, Italian loaf of bread,
Wishbone Salad Dressing bottle she fills with tap water.
Let's go to Teatown Reservation.
I nod as she nudges me toward the car.
We drive to talk radio, I study my new watch.

We arrive.
I carry the picnic up, my feet
crunch leaves,
my mother, behind me.
At the top, rescued animals are in cages.
A skunk has a sign saying he can't spray anymore.
I speak to him in a friendly voice.
Tell him *sorry you lost your powers.*

We sit on rocks.
Mom opens the can with her Swiss Army knife.
Spreads Appetizer on chunks of bread.
We take small bites, pass the water bottle.
Inhale the smoky, wet fall.

On the way down, I collect
rocks and leaves for my pocket.
My mother looks past me.
We drive the empty Taconic Parkway home.
Slowly we pull into the driveway:
broken flower pots, bottles of Piels Beer,
some whole, some shattered.
We go inside.
Couch crooked, coffee table toppled over.
One spindle of the rocking chair rests
on the shag carpet.
Dad, asleep in his Easy Chair.
On the television screen, Audrey Hepburn
pulls on her long, white gloves.

SELF PORTRAIT, AGE 3

This is what I know:
No easy escape.
Feet on flagstone, crossed in third position,
beast in my own yard.

No easy escape.
panting its fetid stench,
beast in my own yard,
its bite is worse.

Panting its fetid stench,
hear the beast snarl,
its bite is worse.
Hair the color of sadness.

Hear the beast snarl.
Eyes flecked with fear,
hair the color of sadness,
yellow gingham sundress, white shy sandals.

Eyes flecked with fear.
Feet on flagstone cross in third position.
Yellow gingham sundress, white shy sandals.
This is what I know.

YORKTOWN HEIGHTS

Everything she makes tastes
of forgiveness:

Orange zest for sweetness
and a handful

of anise seeds, first rubbed between
her palms to remove small twigs,

two tablespoons Italian
news-radio,

half-cup persistence,
an eggshell filled with oil,

The Roman Catholic mass
on television.

The citrusy-licorice aroma
must not be understated.

ACT OF CONTRITION

My best Camp Friend was Liz,
from Rockport. I thought it hilarious
that she lived in a seaside town and went to
camp in a different seaside town.

My sister Laur was my back-up
friend, and it helped because
whenever I was homesick,
I could find her.

Sister Caroline saw me
wave to Janet, the only Black girl at camp,
to sit at our lunch table. Inviting her
wasn't even my idea.
It was Liz's.

They awarded me a gold plastic Christian
Role Model Trophy Cup; it remained dusty
on my shelf for years.

INCIDENT AT ROSETO

It's Sunday and everyone's
tightly in Zio's black car,
mountain spiraling
down to the beach.

Pedal boats, yellow umbrella rows,
Cobalt lounge chairs.
Espresso, cigarettes, the sand man.

There was red;
A balloon
touched down,
in search of meaning.

German soldiers came and
everyone into the wine
cellar trying not to audibly breathe.
soldiers, her
mother's wedding band,
buried under the olive tree.

Sunning myself, I am
surrounded by this war,
our family and the sea.
I catch myself
drifting.

MY MOTHER'S PANE DI SPAGNA

What I wanted
was to become less
neutral.
I wanted to distinguish wet from dry,
sugar and egg yolks,
at low, and at medium speed.
To purify powder from pebble.
In one
bowl: grief
In the other: peaks of strength.
Pour together. Sit and watch
myself through the stained oven door,
flour-dusted in a heap.
Wait.
Pull away from
the sides of that pan.
Rise high above the rim.
Rest before the serving.
Turn
the house upside down.

METRO-NORTH KID

Hop on Metro-North
at Croton-Harmon
to go to *The City*.

The City has its own set of rules:
Jump over sidewalk cracks in red Keds,
run up and down miles of Metropolitan Museum steps,

watch wavy heat lines rise off pavement,
stare up at the Empire State Building,
wonder how King Kong felt up there.

Eat a slice of Ray's Pizza and
yellow mustard on a giant pretzel,
then a hot dog from the cart by The New York Public Library.

Don't touch anything,
keep your eyes cast downward on 42nd Street,
Listen to its soundtrack:

guy shouts *fuck you* out his taxicab window,
swerves as a symphony of horns honk,
(*Steam rises up from underground. Is that hell down there?*)

PARENTING STYLES

My father used to bring me black jellybeans,
those licorice-flavored ones
I hated. I'd shove them
into the back of the nightstand drawer.
Never told him the truth.
He still thinks I love them.

My mother used to bring me apple cider
in fall at college. I stashed gallons
in the bottom of the closet.
Never shared it, never drank any.
Couldn't bear the shame of
leaving her behind at home
with my father and his gallons
of Chianti.

Today I bring animal crackers home for my daughter, Ana,
I tell her we both need
a break from the monotony
of generational anxiety.

IF I KNEW WHO

I would kill him.
A hand sealed my mouth.
My tears, pitch black
A monster with blank face

in the cellar of silence.
my mouth shaped a scream
A monster with blank face,
someone is coming.

my mouth shaped a scream.
my breathing turned shallow,
someone is coming,
I know this like *ring-around-the-rosie.*

my breathing turned shallow.
my tears, pitch black,
I know this like *ring-around-the-rosie.*
I would kill him.

WINTER POLAROID

Up to our waists in a snow drift, me, Traci and D'oro, our golden retriever. Hair smashed under woolen hats, sweating in heavy snow pants and heavy mittens, hurts to breathe the cold. Toboggan sticks out from the snow, next to the old climbing Oak behind us. Someone tells us *Smile*, (these photos never contain adults) snaps the picture, waves it in the air to help it develop.

SPRING POLAROID

In front of the empty mantle we sit on an upholstered dining room chair, my Nonni in black dress and cat eyeglasses and me on her lap, all in white, a tiny wedding dress complete with veil and jeweled tiara: my First Holy Communion dress. My bangs are freshly cut and I grasp the mini bouquet, white with a pink rose center. We smile stiffly and glance to the right, where my mother stands with the camera, listen for instructions.

SUMMER POLAROID

Inside the doll carriage: my new toy poodle, Jolie, and a satin pillow. Traci stands next to that doll carriage, her black curls tied back by an elastic with red beads. We think Jolie loves to ride in that thing, all blue velvet with buttons. Traci places her hands on the handle grip, straightens up a bit in front of the green pachysandra backdrop. Smile, I tell her as I produce my parents' camera. Traci glances up at me. No grown-ups in frame.

FALL POLAROID

My hair peeks out from behind the plastic princess mask. In my arms, a small pumpkin with a crooked stem. The satin dress beneath the pink plastic princess cape is the one I've worn for All Saints Day and our pilgrim play. (My mother is practical and likes to save time.) I stand next to the bare white porch swing, its cushions have already been stored for winter. Behind me the sliding glass doors contain a reflection of my sister, the photographer, in red knee-high socks.

MY GRANDPARENTS: ANGIE AND FRANKIE

They marry young
in Harrison, New York
by the Justice of the Peace,
move to the projects of Astoria.

Frankie retires early due to his back injury,
spends most days learning versions
of solitaire and making lists.
He cleans, he shops.

He whistles a tune while dusting,
hums while eating his sandwich
plateless, over the sink.
Angie, (P.S. 234's favorite cafeteria lady)

gets her hair set in curlers
every Saturday at the Salon.
On Sundays, a trip to see Rita, Jimmy and the kids in Westchester,
their green Duster filled to the roof

with *the sausage you can't get,*
Italian bakery boxes tied up
with red and white string,
a box of wrapped sporks, government cheese,

leftover miniature cereal boxes from Angie's school.
You're the cream in my coffee,
You're the salt in my stew, Frankie croons.
Until the day cigarettes press her lungs to ash.

LIFE ADVICE FROM MY MOTHER

You need some good
decaf black coffee

You must never allow
a knife to meet lettuce

Pieces of anything should be no
bigger than the tip of your pinky

Don't smash the dough or the cookies will be
like hockey pucks

You should always blanch fresh green beans
have them on hand

Go to the Italian deli and buy
a couple of anchovies

Use Crisco
it softens

You want it light
do not use paste

Keep a-i-r-y, don't pack it
or it will taste like sawdust

Weighing down eggplant
gets rid of the bitter

Relationships are like flowers
ignore them and they die.

POEM WRITTEN BY MY GRANDFATHER

All her coats smell like this,
mothballs and Jean Naté After Bath Splash.
I open our shared closet,
the lonely scent is blinding.

Mothballs and Jean Naté After Bath Splash.
I shut our closet tightly,
the lonely scent is blinding.
open again, briefly breathe her in.

I shut our closet tightly,
can't donate her clothing.
Open again, briefly breathe her in,
her scent permanent on the faux fur.

Can't donate her clothing,
it would be wrong on someone else.
Her scent permanent on the faux fur.
No one from church is fit to wear her coat.

It would be wrong on someone else.
I open our shared closet,
No one from church is fit to wear her coat.
All her coats smell like this.

CHRISTENING HEIRLOOM

After the relatives drank the last drops of Crown Royal Whiskey,
my grandmother washed the bottle out, soaked it until its label fell off.
Polished, etched crowns surrounded its neck,
diamond patterns made a crown,
the shape perfect for Nonni's fingers to grasp.

Mom, Nonni and I cooked together, sometimes all day.
Mom took the bottle down from the cabinet above the stove,
Nonni got the metal funnel and Bertolli Olive Oil Can.
I held the bottle steady while Nonni poured the green stream
through. Never spilled any.
Sealed it with a wine cork.

The bottle prepared pans for meatballs,
pizze frite, eggplant parmigiana, streak pizzaiola.
When I moved into my first apartment, my mother
sent it with me, saying
You'll need this now.

MY MOTHER'S PANE DI PASQUA

This one is different, requires half-dozen eggs.
When it's warm with hints of spring

we comb the stores for anise seeds,
select oranges by strongest fragrance.

Make sure the water is tepid,
start to proof the yeast.

Ingredient order can make or break this.
My siblings and I joke, *The higher the bread, the closer to God.*

We all,
with our Mom and Nonni before that,

perform our ritual each year
Wait for it to rise. Punch it down.

Roll out the orange flecked dough,
Carefully cut hand shapes and bunnies.

As we braid loaves,
we chit-chat about little things:

What do you want to be when you grow up?
Purple.

SISTER THERESA'S CLASS, 1977

It's raining at recess
and maybe the nuns
worry we'll get too wet,
and then possessed by the devil.

So it's indoor recess,
No black top today, boys and girls,
the place where we love to chase each other.
A collective *awwww* from the boys,

but we girls secretly look forward
to Sister Theresa teetering
on a chair to reach the dial on the color TV,
mounted right next to Baby Jesus,

holding the Earth in his hands,
and to us it holds exactly the same importance
as the lady on the Don Ho Show
in her hula shirt and coconut bra dancing.

The ad for what's coming up next –
The Gong Show featuring
Chuck Barris
comes on as Sister sits at her desk

and corrects cursive books,
while we sit in our rows,
eat peanut butter sandwiches,
drink milk from paper cartons.

SALVE REGINA

Outside the school nurse's office
the hallway is filled
with nauseating lilac blossoms
and pale me,
hungry and dizzy in my green plaid jumper,
Peter Pan collared shirt.
I sit on the cool linoleum,
clutch my rosary beads,
recover from fainting,
what the nuns call being *moved*
by the grace of Mary, Mother of God,
the treeless blacktop cleared for the May
Crowning,
the metal folding chairs lined
up in rows searing in the sun.

IN THE GARDEN OF MY CHILDHOOD

A tangle of
cucumber tendrils entwines
the trellis.
River rock path
winds through Roma
tomatoes, eggplants sway.
Sunflower heads
bow to rosemary.
Basil harvests pre-autumn
sky as earth
readies itself, rife
with expectation.

FEAST OF THE SEVEN FISHES

My mother sent us three
to Amawalk Seafood
with a list of what she needed.
My brother drove, my sister took the front seat.
I was in the back of the Pontiac,
free of my parents,
clasping the list in my mother's penmanship:

whitefish	*fresh cod*
6 crabs	*2 lobster tails*
shrimp	*smelts*
Baccala	*Squid, with tentacles!!*
2 dozen quahogs	*1 dozen oysters*
mussels	*eel*
Some littlenecks (if they have them)	

Bells jingled on the door as we entered the crowded shop.
My brother waited in line.
My sister and I visited the lobsters in the tank,
felt sorry for their blue rubber-banded claws,
kicked the sawdust on wooden plank floors,
counted lemons in baskets, breathed the brine.

Number 147 was called. My brother spoke for us:
One pound of whitefish, please.
A lady's voice cast across the counter:
That's a Jewish Fish! You don't want that. You want whiting.
I thought of what it meant to be a Jewish Fish.
I didn't know fish had faith.
Wasn't Jesus Jewish, too?
How awkward to visit our Catholic House,
to be eaten there.
It didn't seem quite right. *Get
the whiting,* I whispered to Mike.

PRANZO

IN PRAISE OF VANITY

This morning, a sea hag
startles me
in my bathroom mirror.

She looks
just like me,
crows' feet
frame her chocolate eyes.

She looks nothing
like me,
a purple band
of courage tattooed
on her brow.

She regards me
with admiration,
her flowy silver sea hag hair
determining
my worth.

She looks into me or
maybe it's through me,
all the way to what I
do not recognize
as myself.

TADPOLES

Millions in the shallows,
heaving themselves toward motion.
Some stranded,
some washed up to die.
All of us wanted to help them.
Our fingers drew tiny paths,
road maps for the lost.
We wanted to guide them
to deep water,
but we couldn't
make them
swim.

INDEPENDENCE DAY

We catch fireflies
in cupped hands,
watch them light
like coals in there.
Neighbor boy catches some,
tosses their season
onto the driveway
and with his foot,
makes of them
streaks of iridescence
across black tar.
It is dark and no one
cares where we are.

PASTA SONATA FOR EIGHT

Allegro

Uno a persona, my cousin tells me.
I click each egg under the table,
crack and divide,
let them slide into the center,
take their place.

Andante

I turn the crank slowly on the Atlas Marcato,
it squeaks just a little.
I feed the dough by the slice,
producing long pages of pasta.
Place them under a linen cloth to rest.

Finale: Allegro con spirito

Boiling water awaits each pasta sheet
pressing against the steel strings of the wooden-framed
chitarra until the impression shows through.
I strum the strings, with the back
of my hand, in a sweeping gesture.
It rings out, a discordant twang.

REGARDING UMBRELLAS

My father starts with standard black,
curved wooden handle,
manual force.
Then the Humane Society's powder blue –
an automatic yearly freebie.
Eight-panel, deluxe rainbow,
removable shoulder strap.
You never know when you'll need one,
he says.
He gives me polka-dots, black,
compact, full-size and finally:
a giant golf umbrella, with vented canopy,
though I've never played golf.

SKATING RINK

At the top of the hill behind the house
is where you built it,
measured the space, sketched it out.
You are the daughter whose father gave you this gift.

It's the perfect spot, you said.
Maybe it's because you can see
just over the house to treetops, to sky.
Maybe it's just on the edge

of your memory, the ice rink from
your childhood front yard,
put together with his hands holding
the water in until it froze.

You spent hours getting our rink ready,
so we have the evenings
gliding with our girls,
under halogen lights reflecting snow.

At times I'll sigh when I call you,
your green hooded sweatshirt bobbing
on the hill checking the ice, smoothing
it with the squeegee, patching its leaks.

But the truth is I admire your inheritance –
the drive to create, to repair.
You'll attach that garden hose to the laundry sink,
turn it on full force, run outside in five degrees to tend it.

And when I curse the coiled hose
on the kitchen floor as I trip over
it every morning to get our coffee,
don't be fooled.

FIRE PIT

You build it from stones you find in the woods behind the house and it reminds me of my Nonni whose 107th birthday it is on this night during the first week of autumn we're seated on wooden benches around it

we find green sticks and
your pocketknide, we
and the spicy scent
and ash soaks
times our eyes
wind shifts and
the wrong way.
with my 10-year
and your 5-year
wants nothing but
house in the dark af-
of those Septemnber days, 85

you sharpen them with
toast marshmallows
of burning wood
our clothes., At
sting when the
the smoke blows
We make s'mores
old daughter
old daughter who
to race around the
ter the day has been one
degrees. The evening chilly

enough for sweatshirts, but you insist we wear flip-flops because soon our weeks of winter will begin and our fire will have to move indoors

LOVE POEM FOR BEST

You produce a pocketknife
from the left side of your painter's jeans,
gesture for the fruit bowl.
We sit side-by-side in the kitchen,
my knee presses yours.

You select the pomegranate,
silently hand it to me.
I cradle and study it:
the stem a six-pointed star,
its skin taut with ripeness.

 You hum softly,
as you slice into the shimmer,
break apart the jewels,
offer a cluster to me–
yourself,
your crimson chin.

ANOTHER LOVE POEM

We are neither still nor sweet.
— Paul Nemser

I build trust with my students,

    You build a deck from Trex® decking.

I sit low in a child-sized chair,

    You balance your femininity high on your ladder.

I reteach syllable types: open, closed, silent e,

    You repair the client's ceramic tiles.

I cover Kindergarten recess,

    You cover antique furniture before painting.

I walk a first grader to the Nurse's Office.

    You walk the job site with Faye the electrician.

I hear kids sing along with cleaned-up versions of pop songs,

You listen for the part to hum in the dishwasher.

I watch a class while Ms. Laughlin runs to the bathroom.

You watch how-to videos on septic pumps.

I roll my book-stacked cart.

You drive your truck and tools.

NO NEED FOR ALARM

I left the space heater on all day.
By now the curtains must have caught
fire, the whole house engulfed,
the milk carton I left out on the counter, spoiled.
Cookbook pages blackened Filo dough
The walls buckling, involuntarily
Fire trucks can't turn
on our too-narrow street.
Neighbors gawk
from their front doors:
How could anyone
have been so –

AMERICAN STUDIES IN SIENA

You didn't understand
Italian well enough,
thinking a *mezzanotte*
meant some time,
not promptly midnight

so you got double-locked out
of our barely-been-there-for-a-week-dorm
and I felt forced to wake our
advisor to let you in
after hearing you call over and over

though I'd already counted
the cracks in our ceiling's fresco,
all that time
dreading, the way I used to dread
my father coming home drunk

stumbling through streets
his drunken, pleading voice,
mom's chicken dinner covered in tin
foil kept warm, oven on low
until he made his bad appearance.

AUBADE FOR MY FATHER

The spirit of Sunday
shakes the stained-
glass windows.

Empty booths rehearse
for the coming Strawberry Festival
in the shadows of dawn.

Morning glories cling to the fence,
spirals tightly bound until their time.
Pheasant chicks call out for

pillows, near the sunflower-brushed barn.
I count on the reverence of rabbits
lounging in green-berry fields.

The Zion Church organist repeats
the refrain.

FROM THE CLOSET IN THE SPARE BEDROOM

She has pulled out my Holy Communion dress,
says she's thinking of making pillows from it.
I say *Mom! Please don't cut it,*
keep it for Ana, for when she has children.
My mother continues rummaging through Nonni's leather trunk,
the giant clasps lugged onto the ship from Italy.
Stops at her aunts' trousseau,
the handmade sheets and linens,
the delicate cornered tatting,
the off-white and white
crocheted bedspreads.
And underneath, a green corduroy dress
among the neutrals,
covered in animals: giraffes, monkeys, elephants.
I am surprised.
My mother says she wore this on the ship to America.
She takes it from me gingerly,
to hold against her torso.
Does she want to make it fit again?
Cousin Rina sewed it for me, my mother says,
wistfully tucking her heirloom
back under the tablecloths.

50TH BIRTHDAY

When I'm awake,
I perseverate
on my piccolo pawned for grocery money,
orchestra I never joined,

an unread Sherman Alexie poem,
Dateline NBC,
the last of the honey
from my friend's bees,

And still, I am immobilized by
fluorescent grocery store lighting,
particular playlists,
the scent of wooden wine boxes.

The shrapnel of childhood,
that pressure cooker.

ELEGY FOR MY COUSIN

i.m. Lisa Love 1966-2006

After the Deaf Softball League tournament
the motel lobby is packed, players and fans
stand in groups, wave arms, hands,
fingers at me, as if I understand.
You're here, all the way from Council Bluffs,
a devoted fan to your Omaha team.

I can hug you and fingerspell *hello* with the ASL alphabet.
But it takes too long to spell out each word.
My pencil slips from my hand,
bounces and clatters on the tile floor,
rolls to stillness.

We won!!! You scrawl on my yellow legal-size pad,
the one I carry because I don't know
your Language.

AMAWALK HILL CEMETERY: VISIT NO. 198

i.m. Giovanna Iachini (1906-1978)

Through the gate, the Quaker stones –
names and numbers rubbed smooth by
midnights.

The row of babies' graves, headstones
so tiny, I always slow down.

The next long row is endless with flowers,
a rusty empty vase dug into the ground.

I wander the hundreds, evidence
lined up like dominoes and
tap one, imagining their orderly collapse.

By the weeping willow tree,
I kneel in summer grass,
press my face to earth,
inhale the fresh-cut.

I know I'm close when
beside me is the life-size angel
monument: Robin Berardi.

Soon, I'll find my Nonni's
flat, unmarked grave.

EASTER LUNCH

We're examining the damage the rabbit has done.
My sister whispers
Everything
tastes bitter right now
and I don't know why.
As words exit her lips, I
wonder if we tasted the same thing when
we split that last piece of ricotta pie.
Maybe she tasted the bitter orange,
while I tasted the sweet cheese.
It could be
menopause
or something.
I nod,
like a new car or
a vacuum cleaner.
She leans away from me,
like a bowing sunflower,
and I wonder where she's gone.

UNDELIVERABLE

i.m. Madeline S. McEneney, 1969-2020

Occasionally I text my
dead friend.

*I wish
you were here.*

I send up a signal.
You won't believe what happened.

I wonder if the messages
land there,

or maybe we and our words fall
away from the Earth's surface,

become part of the universe,
linger there.

DISEQUILIBRIUM

I lug the Sony stereo
out to the living room
to listen to Sherman Alexie's mother-memoir
and undecorate the tree.
Those ornaments, crumbled
salt-dough memories
on thin wires.
I'm careful not to drop Jesus
or the Kodak tinsel star,
as I consider both our mothers –
his Native American and mine Italian,
storytellers reinventing family
history to suit their own purposes,
swaddling their babes in layers
of guilt,
hustling us away from drunken fathers.
Their lingering emptiness.

A FREEZING SUNDAY IN MAY

And what can I do but mentally
plant my vegetable garden,
I daydream tomato plants, Boston lettuce,

Japanese eggplant, sweet potatoes, rosemary bushes.
Mentally, I rake the garden beds.
Mentally, it's 65 degrees, perfect for planting.
A slight breeze ruffles the grass in my...

An interruptive alert from the *New York Times*
on my phone: Tyre Nichols'
autopsy shows he died of head injuries
from police beating.

Elaine on my Neighborhood Alert app is worried
about hurricanes.
Doesn't hurricane season start in June?
She texts *we should*
prepare for anything...

WHILE GARDENING

In the woods behind our house,
grief grows wildly,
all the lush and heart-shaped leaves I need.

Grief embeds itself
into the root systems of strawberry plants,
takes every inch of earth,
tries to strangle the perennials.

I gently gather the strawberry plants at the base
with my left hand and tease out the clumps of
grief with my right.
I pitch that grief hard,
toward my bucket.

FARMER'S MARKET, GRATZ, PENNSYLVANIA

No one minds the long lines
for fresh-squeezed lemonade,
strawberries, shoofly pie.
No one looks at a watch.

Amish kids puddle-jumping
in the parking lot, girls gathering
skirts to keep from getting wet,
boys barreling across concrete.

We stand, eat carnival food for dinner:
sausages, hand-twisted pretzels,
catfish on Wonder bread,
Troutman's French fries.

I grasp Ana's hand and we rush
to where girls in bonnets and boys in suspenders
let us taste this sweetness,
wish us good night.

TAROT CARDS

Temperance, framed on the trattoria wall,
i tarocchi minus the winged arcana.
We order wild boar, *pizza con l'uovo,*
a decanter of wine to share on a bench with strangers
until we are full.

From my mind, I draw a card: Courage
cross the Ponte Vecchio,
toss into the Arno, one by one my many
moods: purple, blue, white, we watch

the tourists in the Uffizi courtyard
pose smiling next to the twin
of Michelangelo's *Davide:* both of us could pass
for real in this crowd.

Unbridled the church bells of Santa Trinita,
rise from the river's affection,
at ease, singing effortlessly home.

At Bar Ortensia,
empty both of my pockets,
make room for joy.

PROVINCETOWN

I was in the kitchen
making sauce, garden tomatoes
simmering in their well of loneliness.

Or was I dancing
barefoot on the schooner *Hindu*,
watching the coast soar by,
playing flute on the quarterdeck.

I know I walked through Provincetown.
I drove.
I flew.
Eggs Benedict at Café Edwige.

Did I lose myself at the Song of Myself
Gallery, among the intimate
photographs of strangers?

I know I am somewhere
between earth and sky. I think.

I TEXT MY SISTER

I text my sister
I'm looking for a grief support group.

Only she misses the "grief," texts back
For which family issue?

Children of abusive alcoholic parents,
Children of narcissistic parents,
Children of mothers with Borderline Personality Disorder,
Children of European mothers who encountered Nazis,
People with Post-Traumatic Stress Disorder, anxiety
disorder, panic attack disorder...?

I text back:
Yes.

AFTER SCHOOL LESSON, LEXINGTON MONTESSORI SCHOOL

We're leaving the school
when it catches your eye.

A huddle of five shimmering rabbit kits,
huddled against the building,

like dew drops on morning grass,
still, save for breath in, breath out.

At the corner, the mother rabbit,
brown fur fanned out,

red stain on bark mulch.
I grasp your small, sweaty hand,

hurry you away. You say,
Mama, let me pet him...

IRREGULAR ODE TO LOUD
INTERNAL DIALOGUE

Morning fragmented
worries oscillate my temporal lobe.
That decorative dress that
shouldn't be in the dryer,

my elderly mother's fascination with
Lady Gaga's stolen French
bulldogs, medication in assorted colors.

At lunch our
hummingbird feeder hangs empty,
forgotten, frozen to the hook.

For dinner:
death from cancer,
COVID, the common
cold.

Voluminous language,
unceasing patterns.
And even in my dreams,
I will never be silent.

A FEW BRIEF COMMENTS

I carefully comment on sticky notes only,
make no markings on the child's original page.

The words of my students are sacred.
Red pen is not for children's work.

Green or purple ink,
sometimes gold.

They do not need my loud adult opinions,
nor admonishments to *show, don't tell*.

WHEN SPRING TURNS BACK TO WINTER

To what purpose, April, do you return again?
— Edna St. Vincent Millay

1.

I hear bird songs layered
in the morning air.

First the mourning dove,
the chickadee's staccato notes.

White all over the feeder with a
dollop of red –
the cardinal.

When spring turns back to winter
in April,

birds and flowers
become confused.

How will I become myself,
whispers the wind.

2.

When I go to the window
the male cardinal is not alone.

He glances toward his mate
standing on her empty feeder.

Hears her song, gathers up as many seeds
as he can muster and flies

over to feed her,
from his beak to her

beak. Mesmerizing
this patch of heaven.

AND PERHAPS IN THE SPRING

Eastern Bluebird sings
the sky a chubby royal blue, flush
with brick-red breast, dips
his beak into suet,
announces his claim, more
querulous than joyful.

CENA

UNDER THE CENTERVILLE BRIDGE

We echo our arrival
to overhead kids
before they cannonball into our river,
we dodge the guitar-string fishing lines.

Ana peels water with her paddles,
clicks her tongue at me as
I kayak in circles:
Poor Mama. Need help?
I shake my head firmly, an attempt at confidence,

and my daughter leads us back to the salt marsh
where she holds the boat for me as I climb out
in my muck-shoes, carry our kayaks.
I haul mine, give it everything I have,
worry through the mire.

LADY LIBERTY

The wretched refuse of your teeming shore.
— Emma Lazarus

I am tired
of sweaty tourists,
surveying my seven
crown rays reaching
up to celestial blue.
93 meters above
New York Bay.

I am stressed
by hundreds
of stairs,
narrow and steep,
a metal framework,
a double
helix of loneliness.

I am desperately bored,
staring at Brooklyn,
hearing children's echoes.
I want to reposition
my hands, to play
the guitar,
to sit down.

TO: SCHOOL BOARD
RE: REMOTE TEACHING, FALL 2020

It may appear ideal to teach students from my home,
but keep in mind I'm actually sitting here alone.

No laughter up and down my halls, nor quirky comments said.
No colleagues to exchange a look, I've got my dogs instead.

Dread for my in-school teacher-friends, our overload of tech,
it's hard to keep politics hidden, emotions in check.

Fact is that most of us would do anything for our kids,
but why should it include contracting COVID?

Remote: Far apart in space, says dictionary.com,
the space between doesn't feel like freedom.

SOURDOUGH

Until I feel like a happy Sisyphus.
— Linda Pastan

I feed my starter every day:
50 grams water, 50 flour.
Until we go

out of town and I forget
about my starter –
I should have fed it flour

and water before we left –
at the back of the fridge.
Six months later, we return home.

I rush to examine the spoiled starter,
way past sourdough.
Pink mold streaks,

some kind of bacteria,
not fruity, fresh nor yeasty –
instead it reeks of vinaigrette.

I must throw it away, begin again.

Mom says *never throw food away*.
So I leave it

in the back corner of the fridge:
it's actually still sitting there.

AT THE MIDDLESEX COUNTY COURTHOUSE

I clutch the form,
wait to file a request
from the Paternity Department,
only there's no paternity here.
My ex-wife 9 months delinquent
in Child Support payments.
Deep breaths as I watch
for the next opening in the Divorce Line.

Nightmares fill the notebooks
next to my bed.
I inhale and exhale.
It's my turn and I'm
questioning my rights.
The clerk's accent confuses me.
Dismissed or missed?
She means my case
or is it me?

POEM WITH NO REGRET

It's the one with blooming
irises and beebalm behind
the rocks, between the
moss patches. This is the poem
where I am content
on the patio, facing
the woods, all my
plants carefully selected and
growing with no interference.

No unpublished book, no
unborn children. No failed
orchestral musician, no marine
biologist. No time not
spent with my mother,
my young daughter.
No endless hours handwringing,
nothing about wishes I
had learned to knit,
No desire to skydive, no longing
to be a chef
and a food writer.
No hours revising, recreating
this poem, making it
something it is not.

DECONSTRUCTING THE ASH

Two men in a cherry-picker
begin the work from the highest
point with power-saw,
let each branch drop to the men below,
who stack the wood.
When they get down to the main trunk,
they make a slant-cut and rope it, like cattle,
to control the direction of its
fall. Another power saw
chops trunk into manageable logs.

The last piece of lumber lands,
shaking the house windows,
then silence,
like in church after the priest
says *bow your heads in prayer,*
then the sound of the broom sweep-
sweeping away the sawdust and jetsam,
the same earthy scent of a woodshop.
I go out to measure its trunk –
twenty-four and a half inches across.
tree-guide.com converted it to 33 years.
I begin to count the
rings on the leftover slice

of trunk, but lose count after 13,
hold my hand on the furrowed bark,
wonder what sort of flutes,
softball bats or bows
it may still yield.

What remained looked like *The Giving
Tree* on the page after she gives
everything she has.

PANDEMIC POTATOES

In my mind, my mother's
often shouting something:
You can do so much with potatoes!

So I collect potatoes:
drop into brown paper bags
the red bliss, Yukon Gold,
regular russets and fingerlings.
When they sprout eyes, I bury them
in our garden,
which builds our collection
exponentially.

COOKING WITH MY STEPDAUGHTER

Ellery,
age eleven,
feels driven
to bake
brownies
every week.
She asked for my
help once.

Please, Tru, she sings.
I acquiesce,
agree to be sous-
chef,
watch her
work *from memory*,
I always cling
to recipes,
she always improvises.

She breaks the
eggs, measures
the flour, sifts some cocoa,
cuts parchment.
Recipes are cheating,

Ellery scolds.
She's forgotten
the sugar.

IN THE GAME-ON CAFÉ

plexiglass dividers
vibrate wildly,

barely separate
me from shrill

shouts, whistles, my stepdaughter's *got it*
her friend's *spike it!*

On court 9: the net shimmers
with current research on teaching sight words. (Note: not a metaphor.)

Court 7: my father's shoulder surgery
Court 1: this week's school shooting.

WINTERING

We found the Asian Ladybugs
huddled in a clump in the living room,
in the easternmost ceiling corner.
Ana called it *the meeting,*
As in *how's the meeting going?*
They wouldn't do any harm,
and shouldn't be disturbed –
I looked it up.

The Internet said they were wintering
and if they were thirsty
they would fly toward water.
One morning I found one in the
bathroom, next to the sink.
I put my fingertips under the faucet and
drizzled water droplets
beside it on the counter.
It dipped its tiny head,
a close look showed movement,
tiny antennae twitching, surviving.

Will they make it through?
We filled six small Pyrex water bowls,
placed one by the TV, the plants,

wherever we imagined
they would like to go.

Mama, where will they go?

INVITATION TO TEA AT GRAND RITA'S

Grand Rita gestures for Ana to sit across,
for me to sit at the head.
I admit, I like the decaffeinated black tea
she serves for me.

She has set the dining room table for tea
with unmatched cups and saucers.
Macaroons, instead of my favorite biscotti,
arranged on a blue chipped plate.

Small talk fails.
My mother will not allow much.

We three exchange silences.
My mother who sits at the table stiffly, says
I made macaroons for you,
because I only had one egg.
I stare out the bay window.

Ana takes a macaroon, so sticky between her fingers,
she drops her spoon.
My mother leans across the table, pats Ana on the head,
the way one would pat a dog.
My daughter looks at me.
Time to go
is in her eyes.

MY MOTHER INSISTS ON MAKING CURTAINS

At JoAnn Fabrics,
after I pay for the voile,
she steals a handful of polished, decorative shells
from Indonesia.

They slip from
her hands and rain onto the linoleum,
my mother, shoplifting shiny things.
She bends to grab them,

to shove them into her pants pockets.
Tells me she has a specific vision:
Tell Best to drill
tiny holes in the [stolen] *shells,*

suspend them from clear
wire on the finials,
for those beach cottage curtains,
the ones that frame our view.

CLIMBING WALL

Strapped into the climbing harness,
my daughter's legs poke out like
when I wore her in the Baby Bjorn.

She searches for the rubber pegs with her feet,
grasps them with her hands,
makes her way slowly up,

checks to see that I'm watching.
From 29-feet above, she dangles
anchored to another kid on the ground.

Our matching brown eyes meet.
Her instructor shouts *Touch the ceiling!*
And she does.

POEM WITH NO POET

I'm not scrawling notes
on scraps of paper, not even napkins.

I'm not counting words,
syllables, beats, or lines.

I don't sort through dozens of drafts,
nor try a *glue job* or pantoum.

I don't carry a notebook,
or a pen, no extra pencils.

I never whisper words
to test them out.

A CENTO

This is my letter to the World,
my enemy,

a poem with no images.
trauma with an endless tail –

at night, ocean separates herself from sky by sound alone,
poetry suffering,

lost in the corridor,
consolation gathering like wind

falling from the cloud where I've been gathering,
I hold something back all the time.

Some of us hang on
with tender Majesty,

a leather-bound edition of ourselves,
the gray smell.

Doesn't anyone remember the formula for prayer?
Faith is the fulcrum on which ice turns,

the simple news that Nature told,
a fragment of something.

In the city when you can't see a single star,
flashing her steel-gray eyes,

the darkness burns through,
alone in the village of unsolicited advice.

Judge tenderly – of Me.
Hands I cannot see,

the mystery that holds
sky turns the color of melons.

Sources: [Emily Dickinson, Barbara Helfgott Hyett, Eric Hyett.]

SPLASHDOWN, AUGUST 2020

As Bob and Doug float in the Gulf
of Mexico and Mission
Control entertains phrases like
nominal trunk separation
and nosecone closure,
terminal velocity and altitude
determination devices,
my sister texts
It ain't summer til
you have space and hurricanes.

My brother texts
Just did a quick calculation:
at 17,000 mph if the astronauts
were traveling from Boston
to California, it would take 11 minutes.

Reentry wreaks havoc
on the vestibular system.
Perhaps Bob and Doug confided
misgivings about their return to Earth.
Chaos, human hatred,
germs, Donald Trump.
I can't tear my eyes
away from nasa.gov

REVENANT

i.m. Madeline (1969-2020)

You look up confused: *What are you doing here?*
I live here, I tell you.
We're sitting across from each other in my living room
I can hear Best in the back bedroom building something.
She tells us, *enjoy your chat.*
I know this won't last long so I rush to tell you that I saw a psychic because you
died unexpectedly and I need to know.

You ask if I ever found that Fudge Town cookie that vanished under the couch.
You start to flicker, like an old TV not quite tuned in,
I need to turn the dial.
But
there
is
no
dial.

LEARNER'S PERMIT

Ana adjusts her mirrors,
shouts *Dumbass!* at the driver who cuts her off.
On Route 2,
in the passenger seat, I unwrap
an orange Tootsie pop to soothe my anxiety.

I whisper
*I can't believe you're driving me past
Lexington Montessori School,*
as we pass Ana's preschool.

I'm focused on an idea of heaven,
the sun with rays splayed
behind clouds,
where Nonni lived
after she went to heaven,
or rather Nonni's idea of heaven,
such as high-quality meals
served all day.

Ana murmurs,
Good job, Mother,
as I release the grab handle,
readjust the seat belt,

resist the urge to post
the picture I sneak to take of her
behind the wheel.

FIRST SEMESTER FRESHMAN YEAR

My daughter drives my car
on Route 2 East,
we're en route to Alewife Station,
to drop her off,
her return trip to college.
When we arrive,
she says *I can't go now. There's something wrong.*

I grant her permission to turn
the car around, to head back
on Route 2 West. I say
I'll bring her back
the next morning. At home,
our family greets her without
surprise, without confusion.

GAP YEAR

It's too dry, my 18-year-old accuses.
Ana was actually talking about my
bread and not my propensity to
inflict consequences for being
late. The wet towels
on her floor make me crazy.

Ana's consequences involve work
at a preschool. Anything
to keep out of trouble.
Today's assignment: infant
room. *Babies do nothing, Mother.*

Her departure for college
was only six months ago; I
wrapped her crystal and tiny Buddha
statue, packed a bag full: ramen noodles,
trash bags, Windex and
Mint Milano cookies. A flashlight, too.
(I gave her safety. She threw it in the desk drawer.)

When she was four
she wouldn't leave us either.
They taught us how to hold her tightly

to soothe her, to keep her from getting hurt.
No way she would go quietly
to preschool. Or anywhere.

PURPLE HAZE

And try to stay calm. Smoke days are stressful and an upsetting reminder of our overheating planet. — npr.org

The Dow Jones industrial average is up .53%
The Air Quality Alert is up to Code Purple.
My students have 9 days of school left,
as shown by the increase in meltdowns,
both teachers and kids.
And we're breathing in wildfires
descending on us from Canada.
The city is under
an apocalyptic shroud of smog.
I hold my phone up to the sky,
capture the devastation of Earth:
the orange sun suspended,
like part of a set that needs striking.

SOUND BATH AT NICOLETTE'S

I chose the rose quartz
for love and peace
and the glass angel to manifest my dreams and know
I am not alone.

East, the condor,
new beginnings: that was where we all started.

South, the serpent,
purpose & direction: not a fan of serpents. I was raised to believe snakes
are the devil.

West, the jaguar,
detox negativity: I manage to leave behind some anxiety and my tendency
to over-empathize with others.

North, the hummingbird,
wisdom and protection: strength and tranquility combined.

TO MAKE THE DRESSING

Pride Month, 2021

Find a dress. Not the Little Black Dress.
It's flavorless.

Try the teal dress,
pour it into the Good Seasonings cruet

with some olive oil, white vinegar,
and the girl you had a crush on from Panas High.

Paint your nails blue as Buzzard's Bay.
Pour the dressing over a hated event:

a straight wedding, a niece's confirmation.
Throw away all neutral tones.

VIEW FROM THE INN AT MILLS FALLS

Winnipesaukee
solid with a dark shadow
long docks jut frozen
morning solid stretch – appear
to be stoic ice bridges.

On the town green, white
American flag flapping
Early spring smoke-gray
sky, snow squalls on Main Street where
cars skid lazily.

Glass lake etched in frost
lines and dashes show a path
someone's already
traversed, unexpected thoughts
still brown with melancholy.

Mountains outline the
white puffs' imagination.
Near the frozen lake,
makeshift fire pit cradles
memory: charred log remnants.

On the shore two match
each other's movements until
the ice commences.
Black sweatshirt and hat walks out.
She tests out solidity.

We'll stay together
as tree branches point upwards,
crystals adorn limbs,
lonely loons' calling,
fill up our silent spaces.

CLEANING OUT THE SOCK DRAWER

Because it's overstuffed and barely closed,
because I cannot find two socks that match,
upon the bed I dump them all in rows,
begin to sort them, ditch or patch?
Your Snoopy ankle socks, my peds,
your knee-high thermal working socks,
reunite and match all on the spread,
single socks I fling to dust rag box.
Halfway through this task, I'm overwrought.
Overwhelmed by stripes and plaid and hose.
Heave half the socks onto the floor: I'm fraught.
Fold myself into our bed, repose.
Sock puppets wander through my dreams,
pack bags and run away, rebel, it seems.

ST. MARY OF CARMEN SOCIETY ANNUAL ITALIAN-AMERICAN FESTIVAL

Temporary shrine to La Madonna del Carmine
keeps watch over festivities.
She'll be elevated on a platform,
carried in procession through the Sunday streets,
honored with dollar bills affixed to her with scotch tape.

We stand on the sidewalk near the *Dragon Wagon*,
hands brushing gently, as if on a first date.
We listen to the screech of gears,
inhale the peppers-and-onions air,
sway to the live hits,

a blonde baby Botticelli dances
to *Don't You Worry 'Bout A Thing*,
Long-bearded Vietnam vet taps
his foot along with the band.

Olympia Pasquarosa,
Roger A. Marrocco, Sr.,
Antonio and Maria Magni,
and all the Clementes –

their photos, former society members,
suspended on wires above green, white and red
stripes painted on streets
by the Italian-American Police Association.

My stepdaughter and her Fresh Showered teen friends
wait in line for Fresh Squeezed Lemonade,
pretend not to know us when we wave.

One-toothed clerk at the fried dough truck
rasps *Thanks, honey,*
as she hands over my change.

ACKNOWLEDGEMENTS

I am grateful to the editors of the following journals in which these poems first appeared, in some cases, in another form.

Paterson Literary Review Spring 2024, Issue 52: "My Grandparents: Angie and Frankie"

Naugatuck River Review Fall/Winter 2023: "Sister Teresa's Class, 1977"

Frost Meadow Review 2023, Volume 11: "Independence Day"

Superpresent, Winter 2023, Volume 3, No. 1: "Life Advice from My Mother"

Museum of Americana, Issue 28 Fall 2022 "To Make the Dressing"

Furrows, Deep Earth Collection Green Ink Poetry *August 2022, vol II:* "While Gardening"

Ganga Review (Lalitamba) *2022:* "Poem with No Regret"

Nixes Mate Review, Issue 24/25, Summer/Fall 2022: "Splashdown."

San Pedro River Review, Fall 2022, Volume 14 No. 2 : "My Mother Insists on Making Curtains."

Ovunque Siamo, September, 2020, "Pasta Sonata for Eight."

Constellations, Fall 2019, vol. 9.: "Because My Father Was Drunk By Noon."

Lily Poetry Review, Summer 2020, Issue 4: "Incident at Roseto."

Comstock Review, Spring/Summer 2014, Volume 28 No. 1: "My Mother's Pane di Spagna."

Drexel University Paper Dragon, 2024, Summer Issue, "Undeliverable"

"Mother in Objects" *MER Online Folio, Dec. 15, 20211:* "My Inheritance"

Creation Magazine Spring 2024, Issue 04: "Skating Rink."

Ovunque Siamo, August 2024, "Poem By My Grandfather" and "Parenting Styles."

Love and gratitude to my partner and lifetime love, Paula (Best) Robinson. You embody the true meaning of love. Thank you for supporting me through this project and countless others.

Deepest gratitude to my dear friend, Eric Hyett, who read and reread many versions of these poems and helped them on their journey. I will always be grateful to my teacher and friend, Barbara Helfgott-Hyett and to the PoemWorks community for support while I wrote these poems.

Sincere thanks to Annie Pluto and Michael McInnis at Nixes Mate for believing in my work and for the time spent editing and designing this book.

Much love and gratitude to the greatest siblings on Earth: Laur Lamenza-Naylor and Mike Lamenza. You are officially forgiven for dumping water on me while trying to demonstrate centripetal motion in 1973.

I appreciate my children, Ana Lamenza-Sheldon and Ellery Robinson Curtiss. They have spent years providing me with endless material and making me laugh. And have been understanding while I am in workshops or doing readings. Thanks, girls.

Thank you, Shana Hill and Spencer Thurlow for continued support of my work and just being excellent friends.

Thank you, Kristina Watts, for the gift of your photography.

Finally, thanks also to my Friday Free Write group for all the love and camaraderie.

ABOUT THE AUTHOR

Linda Lamenza is a poet and literacy specialist in Massachusetts. She lives with her partner and their children in the Boston area. When she's not teaching, you can find her near the ocean or in her garden. Her work has appeared in *Lily Poetry Review, San Pedro River Review, The Comstock Review, Nixes Mate Review, Ovunque Siamo* and elsewhere. Her chapbook, *Left-Handed Poetry*, was a finalist for Hunger Mountain's May Day Mountain Chapbook Series. She is a member of the Poem Works community in Boston as well as the Italian American Writers Association (IAWA). *Feast of the Seven Fishes* is her first full-length book. Read her previously published work at www.lindalamenza.com

42° 19' 47.9" N   70° 56' 43.9" W

Nixes Mate is a navigational hazard in Boston Harbor used during the colonial period to gibbet and hang pirates and mutineers.

Nixes Mate Books features small-batch artisanal literature, created by writers who use all 26 letters of the alphabet and then some, honing their craft the time-honored way: one line at a time.

nixesmate.pub

Milton Keynes UK
Ingram Content Group UK Ltd.
UKHW030747071024
449371UK00006B/467